MARS

Also by Elaine Landau

ALZHEIMER'S DISEASE

BLACK MARKET ADOPTION AND
THE SALE OF CHILDREN

COWBOYS

JUPITER

LYME DISEASE

NAZI WAR CRIMINALS

NEPTUNE

ROBERT FULTON

SATURN

THE SIOUX

SURROGATE MOTHERS

TROPICAL RAIN FORESTS
AROUND THE WORLD

WE HAVE AIDS

WILDFLOWERS AROUND THE WORLD

ELAINE LANDAU

MARS

A FIRST BOOK
FRANKLIN WATTS
NEW YORK/LONDON/TORONTO/SYDNEY/1991

Cover photograph courtesy of: NASA

All photographs courtesy of: NASA except:
UPI/Bettman Newsphotos:
p. 31; AP/Wide World Photos: p. 32.

Library of Congress Cataloging-in-Publication Data

Landau, Elaine.
    Mars / by Elaine Landau.
        p.   cm. — (First book)
    Includes bibliographical references and index.
    Summary: Uses photographs and other recent findings to
describe the atmosphere and geographic features of Mars.
        ISBN 0-531-20012-4 (lib. bdg.)—ISBN 0-531-15773-3 (pbk.)
        1. Mars (Planet)—Juvenile literature. [1. Mars (Planet)]
I. Title.   II. Series.
QB641.L36   1991
523.4′3—dc20   90-13097 CIP AC

For Bari Braunstein

CONTENTS

CHAPTER 1
The Red Planet
11

CHAPTER 2
The Surface and Environment of Mars
13

CHAPTER 3
Interesting Features
19

CHAPTER 4
Mass, Density, and Gravity
27

CHAPTER 5
Is There Life
on Mars?
29

CHAPTER 6
Space Probes
35

CHAPTER 7
The Future
43

Fact Sheet
on Mars
53

Glossary
55

For Further
Reading
59

Index
61

MARS

Mars as seen by a spacecraft.
A star background has been
added by an artist.

THE RED PLANET

CHAPTER ONE

The planet Mars appears as a rusty red ball in the nighttime sky. Because of its reddish color, the ancient Romans named the planet after their god of war—Mars. In fact, the fighting god's shield and spear are still used as the planet's symbol.

Mars is one of the nine planets that make up the *solar system.* The solar system consists of the sun and the planets, moons, and other objects that revolve around it. Mars is the fourth planet from the sun. Earth, Mars's neighbor, is the third planet from the sun.

Mars is not a very large planet. Its diameter is about 4,200 miles (6,790 kilometers). That makes Mars a little more than half the size of Earth. The only planets smaller than Mars are Mercury and Pluto.

Mars *orbits* (revolves around) the sun as do the other planets in the solar system. It takes Mars 687 days (Earth time) to complete its journey. The Earth orbits the sun in 365 days (one year). This means that a year on Mars is nearly twice as long as it is on Earth. Mars experiences seasons and weather changes as Earth does, but the seasons on Mars last longer.

As Mars orbits the sun, it also spins around. All the planets spin, or rotate, while they revolve around the sun. Each planet rotates around an invisible line through its center called an *axis*. Mars turns, or rotates, once every twenty-four hours and thirty-seven minutes. The Earth rotates every twenty-three hours and fifty-six minutes. Therefore, a day on Mars is just a little longer than a day on Earth.

THE SURFACE AND ENVIRONMENT OF MARS

CHAPTER TWO

There are dry rocky regions on Mars's surface that are somewhat like areas on Earth. However, the plant and animal life that thrive here could not survive on Mars. One reason is that the temperatures on Mars are too cold. For example, the temperature at Mars's south polar cap can sometimes be below −250°F (−157°C). There is also no liquid or running water on Mars—no oceans, lakes, or rivers.

Scientists think that millions of years ago, there may have been large amounts of water on Mars, but now the water supply is either frozen beneath the planet's surface or in the soil and polar ice caps.

Mars's *atmosphere* is thinner than that of Earth.

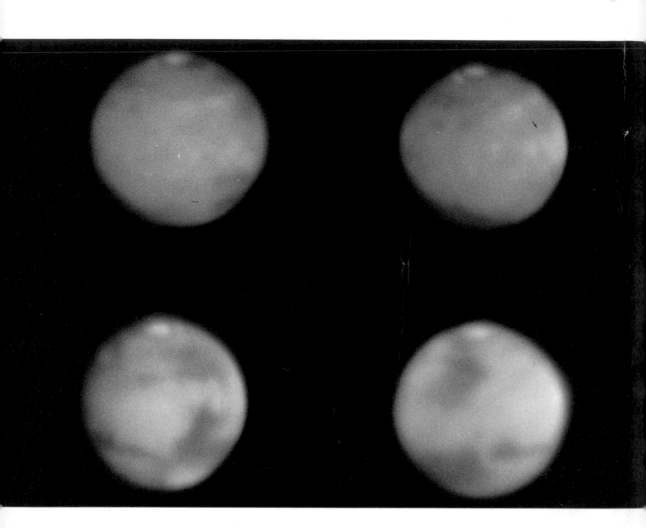

These are four photographs of the planet Mars.
The white spot at the top of each
image is the planet's North Polar Cap.
(The photographs were
taken with a 61-inch telescope.)

It is largely made up of carbon dioxide. The Martian atmosphere also contains small amounts of nitrogen, argon, carbon monoxide, and a few other gases. It has only traces of water vapor and oxygen. Human beings need oxygen to live.

If you looked at Mars through a telescope on Earth, you'd see three outstanding features: bright areas, dark areas, and polar ice caps.

The bright areas of Mars are a reddish, almost rustlike brown. These bright portions make up two thirds of the planet's surface. They are dry areas. In fact, these regions are very much like a desert. Mars's bright areas are dusty and covered with sand and rocks.

Mars's dark areas take up the remaining third of the planet. The dark areas appear in irregular shapes. They are a greenish gray color. These dark areas have been called *maria*. The word *maria* means "seas" in Latin. However, the name does not truly describe the areas, since there is no liquid water on Mars.

The size, color, and shape of Mars's dark areas vary at different times of the year. A portion of the dark area lightens or may even disappear during the planet's fall and winter seasons, but enlarges and darkens during the planet's spring and summer.

A computer-created false-color illustration
of Mars. The turquoise, whites, and yellows
represent Mars's deserts, atmospheric hazes,
and surface frosts. The red color represents
Mars's dark regions.

Astronomers are not sure why these areas change size. Some scientists believe that the differences may be caused at least partially by blowing sand and dust on the planet. Wind storms on Mars can last for several weeks. During these storms, winds may blow up to 100 miles (160 km) per hour. At different times, the sand and dust may cover or uncover the dark areas.

Small areas at the north and south poles of Mars are covered by ice caps. From Earth, the ice caps appear white in color. They contain large amounts of frozen water.

The polar caps also change in size according to Mars's seasons. During the summer, the ice caps melt and grow smaller. At this point, they may give off water vapor. This may account for the small amount of water vapor found in Mars's atmosphere. In the winter, the ice caps freeze and grow larger.

This Martian crater has a diameter of 7 miles (9.6 km).

INTERESTING FEATURES

CHAPTER THREE

The southern portion of Mars is heavily dotted with *craters*. These large holes were probably formed by huge rocks crashing into the planet. The craters on Mars are of many different sizes and shapes.

A large number of these well-defined holes show signs of *erosion*. They've been worn away by time and weather conditions. Some of the craters are actually very old. Some of Mars's craters overlap, and a large number of them have flat bottoms.

A few of Mars's craters are unusually large. One such immense crater is called Hellas Basin. This crater is so big that the entire state of Texas could easily fit inside!

There are also huge volcanoes on Mars. These are located near the planet's *equator* (an invisible belt around the planet's center). Some of Mars's volcanoes are larger than any found on Earth. Mars's tallest volcano, Olympus Mons, is, in fact, the largest volcano known in the solar system. It may be difficult to imagine a volcano of its size. Olympus Mons is three times higher than Mt. Everest, the tallest mountain on Earth. If Olympus Mons were located on Earth, its base would stretch from Chicago to St. Louis. When we remember that Mars is only about half the size of Earth, it's easy to see how remarkable this feature really is.

Mars's landscape may seem breathtaking in some areas. An immense canyon exists in the northern section of the planet. This canyon is called Valles Marineris. In certain places the huge canyon is 124 miles (200 km) wide. It is also four times as deep as Colorado's Grand Canyon. It stretches one-third of the way around the planet.

Scientists aren't sure how the canyon was formed. They think that the land may have been split apart by geologic forces—much like forceful earthquakes on our planet.

Mars's surface also contains areas that appear

This color image of Mars was created by combining three separate photographs taken through color filters. Notice the Tharsis Mountains—a row of three huge volcanoes that appear as three red spots above the surrounding plains.

Above: A model of Mars's largest volcano,
Olympus Mons. The volcano's walls,
shown in the background, tower 15 miles
(24 km) above the plain.
Right: A model of a channel on Mars based on
photographs. It is just one of hundreds of
channels that seem to have been formed by a
broad flow of liquid water.

Phobos—Mars's largest moon.
The close-up view shows the
moon's heavily marked surface.

to be dried-out riverbeds. These regions tend to support the belief of some scientists that considerable amounts of water once flowed on Mars.

Mars has two moons, or *satellites*, that orbit it. Both the planet's moons are small and shaped somewhat like potatoes. The larger of the two moons is named Phobos, which means "fear." At its widest point, Phobos measures about 15 miles (24 km) across. The smaller moon is named Deimos, which means "panic." At its widest, Deimos measures about 9 miles (15 km) across.

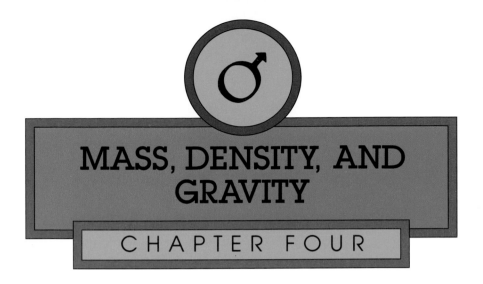

MASS, DENSITY, AND GRAVITY

CHAPTER FOUR

Very often planets are described in terms of their *mass.* A planet's mass is a measure of the amount of material of which it is made. Mars is a smaller planet than Earth. It contains less material. Its mass is only about one-tenth that of Earth.

Density is another way in which planets are measured. A planet's density tells us how compact, or firmly fit together, are the materials which compose it. Earth is the densest planet in the solar system. Mars's density is less than that of Earth. Mars is about a fifth less dense than Earth.

Gravity is a powerful but unseen force that tends to pull objects toward the center of a planet. The force of gravity operates all around us. For example, when you sit down in a chair, you're able to remain there. Your body does not go drifting off into the air. Gravity is what keeps you down. If you toss a coin into a wishing well, it will fall into the water. That's gravity at work as well. Gravity also causes the rain to fall to the ground.

The gravitational force present on Earth operates on the other planets as well. Mars has its own gravitational pull. However, because Mars is a smaller planet, its force of gravity is less than Earth's.

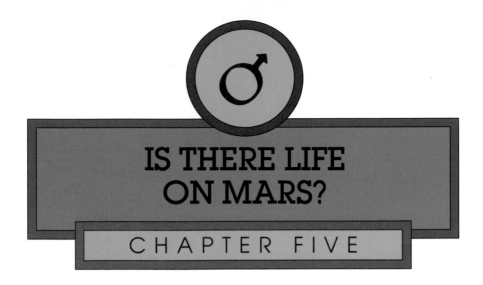

IS THERE LIFE ON MARS?

CHAPTER FIVE

Mars has long been a source of mystery and wonder to people on Earth. Could there be life on Mars? At one point, some astronomers were sure that intelligent life existed there. It all started more than one hundred years ago, in 1877. During that year, Mars and Earth were at their closest points to each other while orbiting the sun. Virginio Schiaparelli, an astronomer in Milan, Italy, took this opportunity to use a telescope and study Mars's surface in detail. He drew charts and maps of his findings.

Among the features Schiaparelli noted were a great many lines streaking the planet's surface. He named these markings *canali*, the Italian word for "channels." Schiaparelli thought that the channels he saw on Mars had to be the planet's waterways.

The following year he published a scientific paper about the Martian channels. As the years passed, he did further research. The Italian astronomer sketched and published a number of maps detailing a complex network of channels. Schiaparelli noted that at times the channels appeared in pairs. In total, he identified 113 channels.

A great deal of public interest resulted from this work. Many people wondered what type of neighbors we might find on Mars. Americans became anxious to know if these waterways had actually been engineered by intelligent Martians.

By 1886, a number of other astronomers had also observed what was thought to be Mars's canal system. Astronomers from the United States, England, and France conducted research on the canal theory. One American astronomer claimed to site dark spots or areas at the base of some canals. He referred to those areas as "lakes."

Still another American astronomer, Percival Lowell, did a great deal to further the theory of engineered waterways on Mars. To complete his research, Lowell built a special facility in Flagstaff, Arizona, which he called the Lowell Obser-

Although Percival Lowell was once a business-man, he later became an astronomer. His theory of life on Mars was disproved, but his later work helped in the discovery of Pluto.

Here Orson Welles performs in the radio broadcast, "War of the Worlds," in which he claimed that Martians had landed in New Jersey. Following this broadcast, Welles later wrote, directed, and acted in numerous Hollywood films.

vatory. Lowell claimed that he was able to identify at least five hundred canals on Mars.

Percival Lowell argued that the canals were not natural features on the planet's surface. Instead, he insisted that they'd been designed and built to meet specific Martian needs. Lowell wrote three books on his theory about life on Mars. He reasoned that Martian civilization was probably in danger because of a serious lack of water. The American astronomer thought that the Martians probably built the canals to bring water from Mars's polar ice caps to its drier areas.

The idea of Martian life was also pursued by science fiction writers. Numerous stories about Martian spaceships landing on Earth appeared in bookstores and libraries across America. In 1938, actor Orson Welles presented a radio play about Martians landing in a small New Jersey town. The broadcast was very convincing. Many people believed that they were hearing an actual news report.

Hundreds of people panicked. Some jumped into their cars and tried to flee from the area. Others locked themselves in their homes. There they waited motionless in the dark, clutching rifles, terrified by the thought of actually facing invaders from outer space.

Although some astronomers claimed that the canals on Mars were real, others were unable to find them. In addition, drawings of the canal systems by many astronomers varied greatly. There were tremendous differences in the widths, lengths, and patterns of the canals, depending on the observer.

A number of astronomers argued that what had appeared as canals were probably nothing more than shadows on the planet's surface. Some suggested that the so-called canals were actually ridges or sand dunes on Mars.

The disagreement about our neighboring planet continued. We were finally able to learn more about Mars as science advanced in related areas. Satellites sent into space yielded much important and useful information about the planet.

SPACE PROBES

CHAPTER SIX

The first successful Mars *probe* was the U.S. *Mariner 4,* launched in 1964. By July of the following year, the probe had flown within approximately 6,000 miles (9,660 km) of Mars. It took some photographs of the planet which it beamed back to Earth. These photos showed that Mars had many craters. Two other U.S. probes to Mars, the *Mariner 6* and *Mariner 7,* were launched in 1969. These probes flew within 2,000 miles (3,220 km) of the planet and revealed signs of erosion.

Important breakthroughs in our knowledge about Mars came in 1971 and 1972 with the probe *Mariner 9. Mariner 9* orbited Mars taking more than 7,000 photographs. It provided scientists with a good idea of what much of the planet

An artist's illustration showing *Mariner 9* in orbit around the Red Planet with Earth and its moon (somewhat enlarged) in the background.

is like. We now had a sort of photographic picture map of Mars. Now the theory of a waterway system built by Martians could either be proven or discarded. At last, a close examination of the *Mariner 9* photographs showed that there were no canals on Mars.

What had Lowell and the other astronomers seen? Perhaps they'd been looking at other surface features of Mars. Maybe the canal system had seemed real to them because they so badly wanted to believe that other intelligent life existed in the universe. It is also important to remember that these nineteenth- and early-twentieth-century astronomers did not have the advanced telescopic equipment presently available.

Some of our best information about Mars was gathered in 1976. That year, two unmanned U.S. spacecrafts, *Viking 1* and *Viking 2,* landed on Mars. On Earth, scientists at Mission Control had planned for the spacecrafts to land on a smooth area of the planet's surface. When they saw the first photographs returned to Earth, they were quite surprised.

Viking 1 and *Viking 2* had actually landed in a rocky region. Some of the boulders in the area were as large as the spacecrafts themselves. Mars's windblown plains are covered with huge

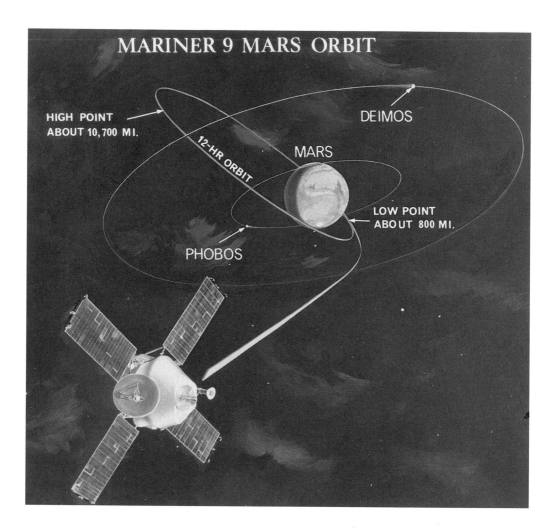

MARINER 9 MARS ORBIT

HIGH POINT
ABOUT 10,700 MI.

DEIMOS

12-HR ORBIT

MARS

LOW POINT
ABOUT 800 MI.

PHOBOS

An artist's drawing of *Mariner 9* orbiting Mars.
In addition to providing information about the
planet, television pictures were also taken
of Mars's two moons—Phobos and Deimos.

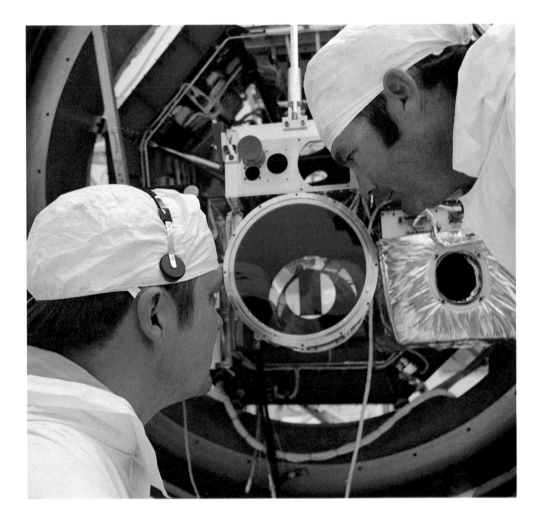

Engineers check the narrow-angle
TV camera of this spacecraft to Mars.
It carried a wide assortment
of photographic equipment.

Here a variety of jagged rocks
and boulders are seen strewn across
an unleveled area of Mars.

sand dunes and jagged rocks. It was fortunate that both landers had settled on small spaces of somewhat smooth turf. Had they hit a large rock or boulder, the *Viking*s might have toppled over and been damaged.

The rich variety of rocks found at the landing sites delighted scientists. Unexpectedly, scientists now had an even better opportunity to learn about Mars. Many of the rocks were a rusty orange color. Scientists later learned that this color was due to iron oxide (or rust). The iron oxide was present in the soil that coated the rocks. In fact, it is tiny dust particles of iron oxide in the atmosphere that give Mars its reddish color.

The rocks were of various sizes and shapes. Some had flat shining surfaces that had been worn down by sand blown about during Martian wind storms.

Scientists already knew that intelligent life did not exist on Mars. But they wondered if other forms of life might be found there. For example, might microscopic organisms be present in Mars's soil?

Both the *Viking 1* and *Viking 2* landers carried equipment to help answer these questions. Mechanical arms scooped up samples of Mars's rocks and soil, and analyzed them for *microorganisms*. They also tested the material for by-products that might be characteristic of some form of life.

At first, the test results were baffling. There were indications that perhaps some type of biological (life) reactions was going on, but later analysis seemed to offer other explanations. After a careful study of the samples, scientists agreed that they were unable to detect any signs of life on Mars.

Still, all the answers aren't in yet. It is important to remember that *Viking 1* and *Viking 2* tested samples from only two locations on an entire planet. Besides, we may be about to enter a new era of discovery.

THE FUTURE

CHAPTER SEVEN

It's possible that we won't know for certain if there is any type of life on Mars until the first human investigators arrive on the planet. There's been some excitement in the present space program about a manned Mars mission. But no one is certain when that will take place. Probably the most reasonable date for such a venture is 2020.

Before that takes place, probes would have to be sent up to study the red planet in more detail. The first such undertaking—*ONE, The Mars Observer*—is scheduled to be launched in the near future. Similar probes to investigate the area would have to follow.

Another possible stepping stone to manned exploration of Mars might be establishing a base on

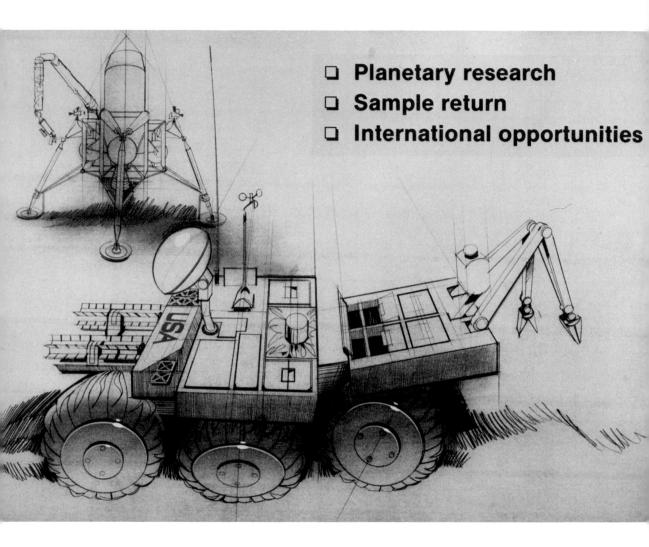

- **Planetary research**
- **Sample return**
- **International opportunities**

Illustration of a possible design for a Mars robotic exploration vehicle.

the moon. Some scientists feel that this could soon be accomplished as well. The lunar base would serve as a testing ground for the equipment needed to eventually send astronauts to Mars.

Even before a moon base could be completed, researchers would have to create a transfer station in space. This is because the large components (parts) needed to build a moon base would be far too heavy to lift from Earth. These massive parts would have to be put together in space.

This station would also be important for the Mars trip. The large bulky vehicle needed to travel across the rocky Martian terrain would have to be assembled at the space station as well. The space station could also be useful for studying the effects of long-term space travel.

Some scientists feel that a single space station may not be the best option. Instead, they've suggested that the necessary tasks be broken down and completed by several smaller units. For example, one station would handle analyzing rocks. Others would be used as assembly and launch points for trips to Mars and perhaps other planets as well.

Here a drawing shows a possible
future means of putting together
massive structures in space.

Like the moon base, these mini-stations would operate for an indefinite period of time. Some researchers feel that mini-stations of this type would be both less complicated and less costly than one large space station.

The space program has already begun work on two new projects that would make space station construction possible. One is an unmanned rocket capable of carrying massive equipment into space. The other is the National Aerospace Plane, sometimes referred to as the "Orient Express." Smaller than a space shuttle, this plane would take off from a runway the same way an airplane does. The plane would deliver astronauts to their destination. Then it would return to its takeoff point.

The costs involved in such an ambitious space program will be high. Some individuals feel the rewards in technological advances and national pride would make it worthwhile. To help lower the price tag on space ventures, cooperation among different nations has been suggested. For example, the Soviets, Europeans, and Japanese all have active space programs. Some people think it is wasteful for scientists in different countries to all be doing the same work. The Soviets have already accepted international help on their Mars probes.

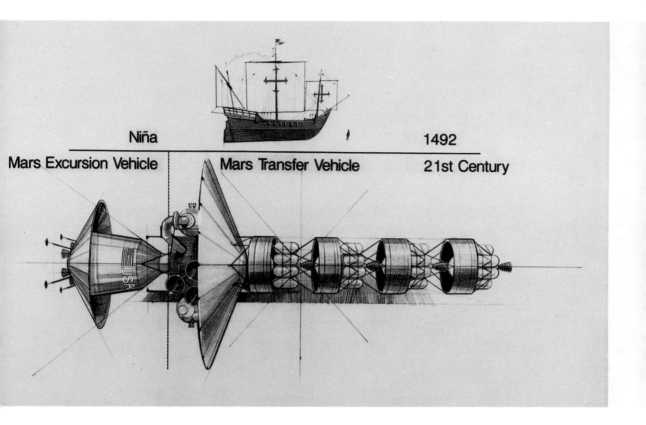

Niña   1492

Mars Excursion Vehicle   Mars Transfer Vehicle   21st Century

This illustration compares the size of a
fifteenth-century ship used to explore
Earth's oceans with a twenty-first-century
ship that might be used in a manned trip
to Mars. The Mars vehicle is divided into
two parts—a Mars shuttle to travel between
Earth and Mars, and another vehicle to
conduct surface operations on the Red Planet.

An artist's drawing of a future
Mars mission. It shows a lander
released from a spacecraft to pick
up Mars soil samples gathered by
a team of robot roving vehicles.

The thought of future Mars missions is exciting. This painting is an artist's fantasy of what it would be like for astronauts to explore the rugged surface of Mars's moon Phobos. Here Mars looms large in the background.

An exciting plan for an international Mars mission was suggested by researchers at our space program's Jet Propulsion Laboratory in Pasadena, California. This mission would ideally take place at the turn of the century—about the year 2000. At that point, French and Japanese satellites would orbit Mars. These space probes would provide detailed surface pictures and communications. At the same time, an American robot rover would comb the planet collecting soil and rock samples. The rover would deposit these samples at specific sites. From there a Soviet lander would pick up the samples and bring them back to Earth. If such a venture were successful, plans for an international manned mission might follow.

Presently, there is support in both the House of Representatives and the Senate for a U.S. Mars mission. President George Bush has also voiced his enthusiasm for the project.

The thought of traveling to Mars strikes an adventuresome chord in many Americans. The United States has long been a nation of discoverers and achievers. Today's dreams may easily become tomorrow's reality. Just think of it—right now you're reading a book about Mars while on Earth. But someday you may be visiting a branch of your library—on the red planet.

FACT SHEET ON MARS

Symbol for Mars— ♂

Position—Mars is the fourth distant planet from the sun. Mars is positioned between the Earth and Jupiter within the solar system.

Rotation period—24 hours and 37 minutes

Length of year—approximately 687 Earth days

Diameter—4,200 miles (6,790 km)

Distance from the sun (depending on location in orbit)—least: 128,500,000 miles (206,805,000 km); greatest: 154,900,000 miles (249,000,000 km)

Distance from the Earth (depending on orbit)—
least: 48,700,000 miles (78,127,000 km); greatest:
248,000,000 miles (399,280,000 km)

Number of moons—2; Phobos and Deimos

GLOSSARY

Astronomer—a scientist who studies the stars, planets, and all of outer space

Atmosphere—the various gases that surround a planet or other body in space

Axis—the invisible line through a planet's center around which it spins, or rotates

Crater—an irregular oval-shaped hole created through a collision with another object

Density—the compactness of materials

Equator—an imaginary circle around the center of the Earth, another planet, or the sun

Erosion—the process of being worn away by the action of wind, water, or other factors

Gravity—the force that pulls objects toward the center of a planet

Maria—dark areas on the planet Mars; although the word means "seas" in Latin, these regions contain no liquid water

Mass—the amount of matter; the body or bulk of a planet

Microorganism—a living thing that is so small it can be seen only under a microscope

Orbit—the curved path followed by one body going around another body in space

Probe—spacecraft carrying scientific instruments that orbits the sun on its way to one or more planets; in doing so, it may fly past a planet it has been aimed at, orbit the planet, or, in some cases, even land there. Planetary probes collect a great deal of data about a planet even from distances of millions or billions of miles.

Satellite—a body, such as a moon, that revolves around a planet; also, a manufactured device launched from Earth into orbit around a planet

Solar system—the sun and all the objects that travel around it; such objects include planets, moons, chunks of iron and stone called meteorites, and even tiny flakes of dust

FOR FURTHER READING

Atkinson, Stuart. *Journey into Space.* New York: Viking, 1988.

Branley, Franklyn M. *The Sun: Our Nearest Star.* New York: Crowell, 1988.

Cobb, Vicki. *Why Doesn't the Earth Fall Up.* New York: Lodestar, 1988.

Lampton, Christopher. *Stars and Planets.* New York: Doubleday, 1988.

Simon, Seymour. *Galaxies.* New York: Morrow, 1988.

Wyler, Rose. *Starry Night.* Englewood Cliffs, N.J.: Julian Messner, 1989.

INDEX

Page numbers in *italics* refer to illustrations.

Atmosphere, 13–15, *16*
Axis, 12

Boulders, 37–41, *40*
Bright areas, 15
Bush, George, 51

Canyons, 20
Channels, *23*, 25, 29–33, 34, 37
Congress, U.S., 51

Craters, *18*, 19, 35

Dark areas, 15–17, *16*
Day, length of, 12
Deimos, 25, *38*, 54
Density, 27
Deserts, 15, *16*

Earth, 11, 12, 13, 20, 27, 28, 29, *36*, 53, 54
Erosion, 19, 35

Gravity, 27–28

Hellas Basin, 19

International cooperation, 47–51
Iron oxide, 41

Jet Propulsion Laboratory, 51
Jupiter, 53

Lowell, Percival, 30–33, *31*, 37
Lowell Observatory, 30–33
Lunar base, 43–45

Maria, 15–17
Mariner missions, 35–37, *36, 38*
Mars, *10*
    atmosphere of, 13–15, *16*
    density of, 27
    distance from Earth, 54
    distance from sun, 53
    fact sheet on, 53–54
    gravity on, 28
    length of year on, 12, 53
    manned mission to, 43–47, *48, 50,* 51
    mass of, 27
    moons of, *24,* 25, *38, 50,* 54
    naming of, 11
    orbit of, 11, 12, 53–54
    possibility of life on, 13, 29–34, 37, 41–42, 43
    probes to, 35–42, *36, 38, 39,* 43, 47, *49,* 51
    reddish color of, 11, 41
    rotation of, 12, 53
    seasons and weather changes on, 12, 15–17
    size of, 11, 53
    surface of, 13, *14,* 15–25, *16, 18, 21–23,* 29–33, 34, 35, 37–42, *40*
    symbol for, 11, 53
    temperature on, 13

Mars (continued)
water on, 13, 15, 17, *23*, 25, 33
wind storms on, 17, 41
Mass, 27
Mercury, 11
Moon (Earth), *36*
base on, 43–45
Moons (Mars), *24*, 25, *38*, *50*, 54

National Aerospace Plane, 47

Olympus Mons, 20, *22*
ONE, The Mars Observer, 43
"Orient Express," 47

Phobos, *24*, *25*, *38*, *50*, 54
Pluto, 11, *31*
Polar ice caps, *14*, 15, 17

Robotic exploration
vehicles, *44*, *49*, 50
Rocks, 37–42, *40*, 51
Romans, ancient, 11

Rotation period, 12, 53

Schiaparelli, Virginio, 29–30
Science fiction, *32*, 33
Soil, 41–42, *49*
Solar system, 11, 12
Soviet Union, 47, 51
Space probes, 35–42, *36*, *38*, *39*, 43, 47, *49*, 51
Space stations, 45–47, *46*
Sun, 11, 12, 53

Temperature, 13
Tharsis Mountains, *21*

Valles Marineris, 20
Viking missions, 37–42
Volcanoes, 20, *21*, *22*

"War of the Worlds," *32*, 33
Water, 13, 15, 17, *23*, 25, 33
Welles, Orson, *32*, 33
Wind storms, 17, 41

Year, length of, 12, 53

ABOUT THE AUTHOR

Elaine Landau received her BA degree from New York University in English and journalism and a master's degree in library and information science from Pratt Institute in New York City.

Ms. Landau has worked as a newspaper reporter, an editor, and a youth services librarian. She has written many books and articles for young people. Ms. Landau lives in Sparta, New Jersey.